AF228491

HOW DO PLANTS GROW?

Annabel Griffin

Illustrated by Tjarda Borsboom

First published in 2024 by Hungry Tomato Ltd
F15, Old Bakery Studios, Blewetts Wharf, Malpas Road, Truro, Cornwall, TR1 1QH, UK.

A CIP catalog record for this book is available from the British Library.

ISBN 9781835690048

Printed in China

Discover more at
www.hungrytomato.com

Contents

Words in **BOLD** can be found in the glossary.

Picture Credits:

Abbreviations: m-middle, t-top, l-left, r-right, bg-background.

Shutterstock: Estragon 19br; Kazakova Maryia 18-19bg; Likar 23mr; Mazur Travel 23br; Nailia Schwarz 23ml; Photoongraphy 23tl; Skrypnykov Dmytro 23tr; Surked 23bl; Will Pedro 21tl; xpixel 20tl.

Every effort has been made to trace the copyright holders, and we apologize in advance for any unintentional omissions. We would be pleased to insert the appropriate acknowledgments in any subsequent edition of this publication.

What Is a Plant?

Plants are living things that can be found almost everywhere on Earth! There are over 300,000 different types of plants on our planet. How many can you name?

Plants come in all sorts of shapes and sizes, but most of them have the same three parts: stem, roots, and leaves.

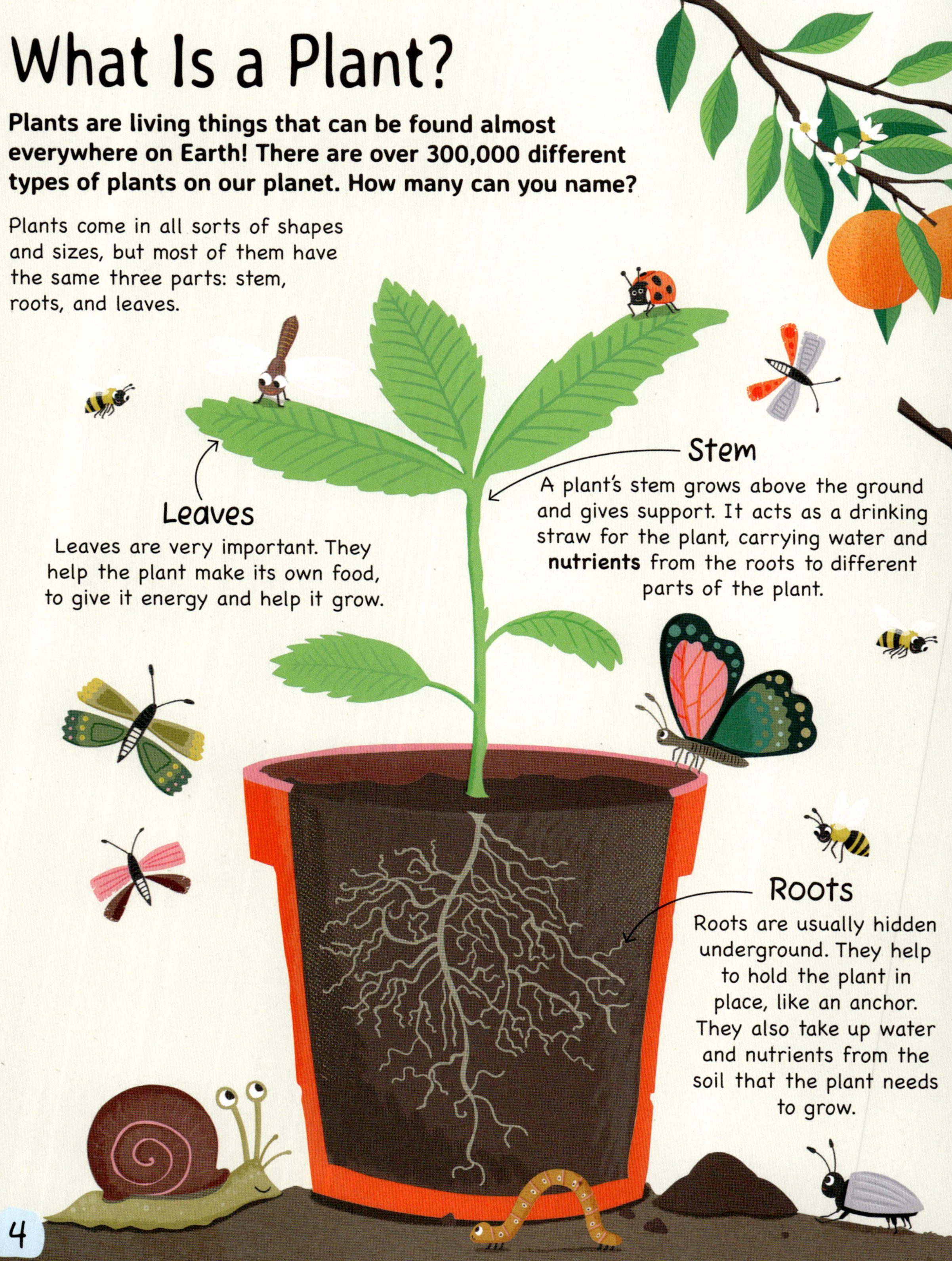

Stem

A plant's stem grows above the ground and gives support. It acts as a drinking straw for the plant, carrying water and **nutrients** from the roots to different parts of the plant.

Leaves

Leaves are very important. They help the plant make its own food, to give it energy and help it grow.

Roots

Roots are usually hidden underground. They help to hold the plant in place, like an anchor. They also take up water and nutrients from the soil that the plant needs to grow.

Blossom
Fruit
Berries
Some plants have other features, such as fruit, flowers, thorns, and branches.
Nuts
Flower
Petals
Thorns
Branches
Trunk

What Do Plants Need?

Plants can't grow without a few very important things: sunlight, air, water, and nutrients.

Sun

Plants take light from the sun and turn it into food, which gives them energy to grow.

Air and water

Without enough air and water, plants will quickly shrivel up and die.

Nutrients

The roots of a plant take up water and nutrients (food) from the soil.

Space

Some plants need space away from other plants to avoid **competing** for nutrients in the soil.

Cactus
By storing water, some plants survive in very hot places, like deserts.
Some plants like water so much that they grow in ponds, lakes, rivers, or oceans.
RIBBIT
Moss
Plants, like moss, grow on other things, such as tree trunks, branches, and rocks.

How Do Plants Grow?

Most plants grow from seeds. Even a
gigantic tree starts its life as a tiny seed.
How does it all begin?

When a seed is planted
and given water, it will
begin to grow into a plant.
This is called **germination**.

1.
A root starts to grow
out from the seed.

2.
A shoot grows up from
the seed towards the
soil's surface.

3.
The roots continue to grow as
the shoot becomes a stem and
starts to grow leaves.

4.
The plant grows bigger and stronger, creating more leaves and forming a flower bud.

5.
The plant reaches its full size and its flower opens.

Let's Grow a Seed
You will need:
- Sunflower seeds
- Large plant pot
- Peat-free potting compost

1. Read the seed packet to find the best time for planting.

2. Fill a large flowerpot with potting compost. Push a seed about ½ inch (1cm) down into the compost and cover it fully.

3. Place it in a sunny spot and water it regularly, so it doesn't dry out.

How Do Bees Help Plants?

Bees are very helpful friends to plants. They carry **pollen** from one flower to another. This is called **pollination**. Plants need pollen from other flowers to make new seeds.

1.
Bees are attracted to a flower's bright petals and lovely scent.

2.
Flowers contain nectar, a sweet liquid that bees collect to make honey.

3.
As a bee collects the nectar, it becomes covered in pollen, which is carried to the next flower it visits.

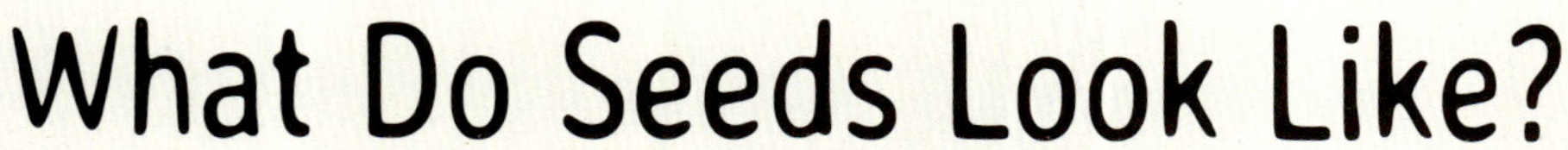

What Do Seeds Look Like?

Seeds come in lots of different shapes and sizes. Some seeds are nice to eat, and some are hidden inside fruit. Have you seen any of these seeds before?

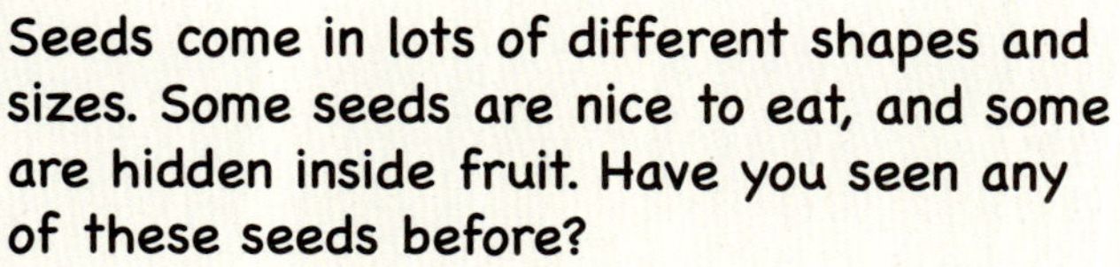

Poppy

Once pollinated, a poppy will lose its petals and grow a **seedpod**, full of tiny black seeds.

The seedpod has holes, like a saltshaker, so seeds can blow out in the wind.

Sunflower

Sunflower seeds grow in the middle of the flower.

Wheat

Wheat seeds are used to make flour. They grow at the top of each stalk.

Apple
You've probably seen the seeds hidden inside an apple.

Strawberry
Strawberry seeds grow on the outside of each fruit.

Cherry
The hard stone inside a cherry is actually a seed.

Walnut
Nuts are also seeds! Most of them grow inside hard shells.

Corn
Did you know that corn kernels are seeds too?

How Do Plants Get Around?

Plants can't move around like animals, so they have to find other ways to spread their seeds.

Seed splat
Some birds eat seeds and poop them out. Watch out!

Sticky seeds
Some seeds have little spikes or hooks that stick to an animal's fur, and get carried away to spread and grow.

Buried treasure
Squirrels bury seeds, storing them to eat in the winter. Forgotten seeds will remain buried and grow instead!

Dandelion seeds

Soaring seeds
Some seeds are blown away
by the wind.

Maple seeds

Coconut

Lotus plant

Swimming seeds
Some plants, like coconut trees
and lotus plants, drop their
seeds into water, to be carried
away by the current.

Hazel

Seed explosion
Some seedpods explode or burst
open, shooting their seeds away
from the plant.

Squirting
cucumber

Amazing Bugs

**Did you spot the creepy-crawlies hidden throughout this book?
Creepy-crawlies are an important part of keeping plants healthy!**

Buzzing bumblebees

Bees are one of the most important bugs. We rely on them to spread pollen, which helps flowers, fruits, and vegetables to grow.

Daring dragonflies

These prehistoric bugs have existed for over 300 million years! Dragonflies love ponds and wildflower meadows, where they hunt plant-eating bugs.

Wiggly worms

Worms are invertebrates, which means they don't have any bones! They wiggle through soil, eating dead plants and leaving behind nutrients for plants to soak up.

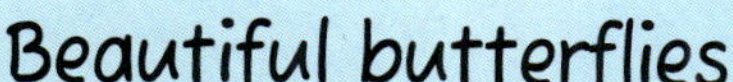

Beautiful butterflies

Butterflies have brightly patterned wings, making them the prettiest bug of all. Like bees, they drink nectar from flowers and pollinate yards and meadows, helping new plants to grow.

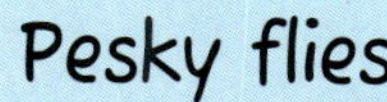

Pesky flies

It's true that some flies buzz around, eating plants, fruits, and vegetables. However, many flies actually help plants grow by pollinating them, just like bees do!

Brilliant beetles

Beetles can be all sorts of shapes and sizes. They are great because they hunt and eat bugs, like slugs and snails, that destroy plants.

Let's Grow Tomatoes

See the magic of plants in action by growing your very own tomatoes! You can grow them outside or in a greenhouse, as long as they get plenty of sun. Ask an adult to help you choose a good place for your plants before starting.

You will need:

- Packet of tomato seeds
- Soil/peat-free potting compost
- Mini plant pots/seed trays
- Medium to large pots
- Tomato feed
- Plastic wrap
- Long sticks (to hold the plant upright)
- Yarn/string

Important tips:

- Always follow the instructions on the seed packet to know when to **sow,** plant, and **harvest** your tomatoes.

- Don't worry if not all your seeds grow – that's very normal. That's why it's important to plant more than 1 seed!

- If any of your plants struggle to stand up on their own, tie the stem to a stick to help the plant out.

1.

Fill your mini pots/seed tray with compost to about ½ inch (1cm) from the top.

2.

Space out 1-2 seeds on the surface, then cover with a thin layer of soil. Lightly water, cover with plastic wrap, and place somewhere warm and light.

3.

In 5-10 days, the seeds should start to sprout. Once you see the plant above the soil, take off the plastic wrap. Keep the soil moist by watering it regularly.

4.

When the seedlings are 3 inches (7.5cm), move them into the medium pots. Hold them by the leaves, not the stems. Water every day.

5.

When flowers start appearing, carefully move your plants into the biggest pots. Now they have space to grow.

6.

Now, put the plants outside or in a greenhouse. Give them tomato feed every week and keep watering them.

7.

The flowers should turn into tomatoes! Be patient while they grow; it can take a few months from sowing the seeds to harvesting the fruit, but it will be worth the wait!

Did You Know?

Plants are pretty amazing! Every living creature needs plants to survive; the world wouldn't be the way it is today if we didn't have them. Did you know these amazing facts about plants?

Bristlecone pine tree

The oldest living plant on Earth is a bristlecone pine tree in California (USA), which is almost **5,000** years old!

A single bee can pollinate over **1,000** flowering plants in one day!

Around **80%** of all flowering plants rely on insects, such as bees and butterflies, for pollination. Where would we be without them?

Match Up the Pairs

**Can you match up the fact boxes (below) with the correct plant (right)?
Flip back through the book if you need a hint!**

1.

My sweet, yellow seeds are called kernels. They are yummy to eat.

2.

I'm a pretty flower. My tiny, black seeds grow in a seedpod after I lose my petals.

3.

I'm a big, tall flower that's yellow, like the sun.

4.

I'm a tree and I like to grow near water, so that my seeds can be spread by the current.

5.

I'm a tree which grows tasty green or red fruit.

6.

I'm a plant that grows sweet fruit whose seeds grow on the outside.

Corn

Sunflower

Poppy

Strawberry plant

Coconut tree

Apple tree

Glossary

Competing – (verb) going against one another to gain or win something.

Current – the continuous movement of a body of water, such as a river or ocean.

Germination – the process when a seed begins to sprout roots and shoots.

Harvest – (verb) the process of gathering in crops when they are ripe and ready to be gathered.

Nutrients – substances or ingredients that plants and animals need to live and grow.

Pollen – a dusty powder made by some plants. It is used within pollination (see below) to produce new seeds.

Pollination – when pollen (see above) is moved from one plant to another – often by an insect – so that the plants can make new seeds.

Seedpod – a pouch or case produced by some plants to hold their seeds.

Sow – (verb) to plant or scatter seeds into soil.

Trunk – the large woody stem of a tree, where the branches grow from.

Answers to Match Up the Pairs

Answers: 1. Corn, 2. Poppy, 3. Sunflower, 4. Coconut tree, 5. Apple tree, 6. Strawberry plant.